CANNABIS GROWERS JOURNAL

D1714945

THIS NOTEBOOK BELONGS TO:

....

....

....

Strain Name:	Method/Technique
Date Started:	☐ Seed ☐ Clone

Marijuana Type: ☐ Indica   ☐ Sativa   ☐ Hybrid

Cannabis Seeds: ☐ Feminized ☐ Autoflower ☐ Regular ☐ CBD

Plant Count	Date Harvested	Date Begin	Date End Cure

AROMA

Bud Density

Loose   50 %   Dense

Trichome Color

White   50 %   Amber

APPEARANCE

NOTES

FEEDING SCHEDULE

	☐ Milliliter	☐ Tablespoon	☐ Teaspoon		
Week #	1	2	3	4	5
Growth Stage					
PPM Range					

NOTES

Reservoir/Bucket Size:				Optimal pH:		
6	7	8	9	10	11	12

NOTES

Strain Name:	Method/Technique
Date Started:	☐ Seed ☐ Clone

Marijuana Type: ☐ Indica ☐ Sativa ☐ Hybrid

Cannabis Seeds: ☐ Feminized ☐ Autoflower ☐ Regular ☐ CBD

Plant Count	Date Harvested	Date Begin	Date End Cure

AROMA

Bud Density

Loose   50 %   Dense

Trichome Color

White   50 %   Amber

APPEARANCE

NOTES

FEEDING SCHEDULE

	Milliliter	Tablespoon	Teaspoon		
Week #	1	2	3	4	5
Growth Stage					
PPM Range					

NOTES

Reservoir/Bucket Size:				Optimal pH:		
6	7	8	9	10	11	12

NOTES

Strain Name:	Method/Technique
Date Started:	☐ Seed ☐ Clone

Marijuana Type: ☐ Indica   ☐ Sativa   ☐ Hybrid

Cannabis Seeds: ☐ Feminized ☐ Autoflower ☐ Regular ☐ CBD

Plant Count	Date Harvested	Date Begin	Date End Cure

AROMA

Bud Density

Loose   50 %   Dense

Trichome Color

White   50 %   Amber

APPEARANCE

NOTES

FEEDING SCHEDULE

	☐ Milliliter	☐ Tablespoon		☐ Teaspoon	
Week #	1	2	3	4	5
Growth Stage					
PPM Range					

NOTES

Reservoir/Bucket Size:				Optimal pH:		
6	7	8	9	10	11	12

NOTES

Strain Name:	Method/Technique
Date Started:	☐ Seed ☐ Clone

Marijuana Type: ☐ Indica   ☐ Sativa   ☐ Hybrid

Cannabis Seeds: ☐ Feminized ☐ Autoflower ☐ Regular ☐ CBD

Plant Count	Date Harvested	Date Begin	Date End Cure

AROMA

Bud Density

Loose   50 %   Dense

Trichome Color

White   50 %   Amber

APPEARANCE

NOTES

FEEDING SCHEDULE

	☐ Milliliter	☐ Tablespoon		☐ Teaspoon	
Week #	1	2	3	4	5
Growth Stage					
PPM Range					

NOTES

Reservoir/Bucket Size:				Optimal pH:		
6	7	8	9	10	11	12

NOTES

Strain Name:	Method/Technique
Date Started:	☐ Seed ☐ Clone

Marijuana Type: ☐ Indica ☐ Sativa ☐ Hybrid

Cannabis Seeds: ☐ Feminized ☐ Autoflower ☐ Regular ☐ CBD

Plant Count	Date Harvested	Date Begin	Date End Cure

AROMA

Bud Density

Loose   50 %   Dense

Trichome Color

White   50 %   Amber

APPEARANCE

NOTES

FEEDING SCHEDULE

	☐ Milliliter	☐ Tablespoon		☐ Teaspoon	
Week #	1	2	3	4	5
Growth Stage					
PPM Range					

NOTES

Reservoir/Bucket Size:				Optimal pH:		
6	7	8	9	10	11	12

NOTES

Strain Name:	Method/Technique
	☐ Seed ☐ Clone
Date Started:	

Marijuana Type: ☐ Indica ☐ Sativa ☐ Hybrid

Cannabis Seeds: ☐ Feminized ☐ Autoflower ☐ Regular ☐CBD

Plant Count	Date Harvested	Date Begin	Date End Cure

AROMA

Bud Density

Loose   50 %   Dense

Trichome Color

White   50 %   Amber

APPEARANCE

NOTES

FEEDING SCHEDULE

	☐ Milliliter	☐ Tablespoon		☐ Teaspoon	
Week #	1	2	3	4	5
Growth Stage					
PPM Range					

NOTES

Reservoir/Bucket Size:				Optimal pH:		
6	7	8	9	10	11	12

NOTES

Strain Name:	Method/Technique
	☐ Seed ☐ Clone
Date Started:	

Marijuana Type: ☐ Indica   ☐ Sativa   ☐ Hybrid

Cannabis Seeds: ☐ Feminized ☐ Autoflower ☐ Regular ☐ CBD

Plant Count	Date Harvested	Date Begin	Date End Cure

AROMA

Bud Density

Loose   50 %   Dense

Trichome Color

White   50 %   Amber

APPEARANCE

NOTES

FEEDING SCHEDULE

	☐ Milliliter	☐ Tablespoon		☐ Teaspoon	
Week #	1	2	3	4	5
Growth Stage					
PPM Range					

NOTES

Reservoir/Bucket Size:				Optimal pH:		
6	7	8	9	10	11	12

NOTES

Strain Name:	Method/Technique
Date Started:	☐ Seed ☐ Clone

Marijuana Type:	☐ Indica	☐ Sativa	☐ Hybrid

Cannabis Seeds: ☐ Feminized ☐ Autoflower ☐ Regular ☐ CBD

Plant Count	Date Harvested	Date Begin	Date End Cure

AROMA

Bud Density

Loose   50 %   Dense

Trichome Color

White   50 %   Amber

APPEARANCE

NOTES

FEEDING SCHEDULE

	☐ Milliliter	☐ Tablespoon		☐ Teaspoon	
Week #	1	2	3	4	5
Growth Stage					
PPM Range					

NOTES

Reservoir/Bucket Size:				Optimal pH:		
6	7	8	9	10	11	12

NOTES

Strain Name:	Method/Technique
Date Started:	☐ Seed ☐ Clone

Marijuana Type: ☐ Indica ☐ Sativa ☐ Hybrid

Cannabis Seeds: ☐ Feminized ☐ Autoflower ☐ Regular ☐ CBD

Plant Count	Date Harvested	Date Begin	Date End Cure

AROMA

Bud Density

Loose   50 %   Dense

Trichome Color

White   50 %   Amber

APPEARANCE

NOTES

Feeding Schedule

	☐ Milliliter	☐ Tablespoon		☐ Teaspoon	
Week #	1	2	3	4	5
Growth Stage					
PPM Range					

Notes

Reservoir/Bucket Size:				Optimal pH:		
6	7	8	9	10	11	12

NOTES

Strain Name:	Method/Technique
Date Started:	☐ Seed ☐ Clone

Marijuana Type: ☐ Indica ☐ Sativa ☐ Hybrid

Cannabis Seeds: ☐ Feminized ☐ Autoflower ☐ Regular ☐ CBD

Plant Count	Date Harvested	Date Begin	Date End Cure

AROMA

Bud Density

Loose   50 %   Dense

Trichome Color

White   50 %   Amber

APPEARANCE

NOTES

FEEDING SCHEDULE

	☐ Milliliter	☐ Tablespoon		☐ Teaspoon	
Week #	1	2	3	4	5
Growth Stage					
PPM Range					

NOTES

Reservoir/Bucket Size:				Optimal pH:		
6	7	8	9	10	11	12

NOTES

Strain Name:	Method/Technique
Date Started:	☐ Seed ☐ Clone

Marijuana Type: ☐ Indica ☐ Sativa ☐ Hybrid

Cannabis Seeds: ☐ Feminized ☐ Autoflower ☐ Regular ☐ CBD

Plant Count	Date Harvested	Date Begin	Date End Cure

AROMA

Bud Density

Loose   50 %   Dense

Trichome Color

White   50 %   Amber

APPEARANCE

NOTES

Feeding Schedule

Week #	☐ Milliliter	☐ Tablespoon		☐ Teaspoon	
	1	2	3	4	5
Growth Stage					
PPM Range					

Notes

Reservoir/Bucket Size:				Optimal pH:		
6	7	8	9	10	11	12

NOTES

Strain Name:	Method/Technique
Date Started:	☐ Seed ☐ Clone

Marijuana Type: ☐ Indica ☐ Sativa ☐ Hybrid

Cannabis Seeds: ☐ Feminized ☐ Autoflower ☐ Regular ☐ CBD

Plant Count	Date Harvested	Date Begin	Date End Cure

AROMA

Bud Density

Loose   50 %   Dense

Trichome Color

White   50 %   Amber

APPEARANCE

NOTES

FEEDING SCHEDULE

	□ Milliliter	□ Tablespoon		□ Teaspoon	
Week #	1	2	3	4	5
Growth Stage					
PPM Range					

NOTES

Reservoir/Bucket Size:				Optimal pH:		
6	7	8	9	10	11	12

NOTES

Strain Name:	Method/Technique
Date Started:	☐ Seed ☐ Clone

Marijuana Type: ☐ Indica ☐ Sativa ☐ Hybrid

Cannabis Seeds: ☐ Feminized ☐ Autoflower ☐ Regular ☐ CBD

Plant Count	Date Harvested	Date Begin	Date End Cure

AROMA

Bud Density

Loose   50 %   Dense

Trichome Color

White   50 %   Amber

APPEARANCE

NOTES

FEEDING SCHEDULE

	☐ Milliliter	☐ Tablespoon		☐ Teaspoon	
Week #	1	2	3	4	5
Growth Stage					
PPM Range					

NOTES

Reservoir/Bucket Size:				Optimal pH:		
6	7	8	9	10	11	12

NOTES

Strain Name:	Method/Technique
Date Started:	☐ Seed ☐ Clone

Marijuana Type: ☐ Indica ☐ Sativa ☐ Hybrid

Cannabis Seeds: ☐ Feminized ☐ Autoflower ☐ Regular ☐ CBD

Plant Count	Date Harvested	Date Begin	Date End Cure

AROMA

Bud Density

Loose   50 %   Dense

Trichome Color

White   50 %   Amber

APPEARANCE

NOTES

FEEDING SCHEDULE

	Milliliter	Tablespoon		Teaspoon	
Week #	1	2	3	4	5
Growth Stage					
PPM Range					

NOTES

Reservoir/Bucket Size:				Optimal pH:		
6	7	8	9	10	11	12

NOTES

Strain Name:	Method/Technique
	☐ Seed ☐ Clone
Date Started:	

Marijuana Type: ☐ Indica ☐ Sativa ☐ Hybrid

Cannabis Seeds: ☐ Feminized ☐ Autoflower ☐ Regular ☐ CBD

Plant Count	Date Harvested	Date Begin	Date End Cure

AROMA

Bud Density

Loose   50 %   Dense

Trichome Color

White   50 %   Amber

APPEARANCE

NOTES

FEEDING SCHEDULE

	☐ Milliliter	☐ Tablespoon		☐ Teaspoon	
Week #	1	2	3	4	5
Growth Stage					
PPM Range					

NOTES

Reservoir/Bucket Size:				Optimal pH:		
6	7	8	9	10	11	12

NOTES

Strain Name:	Method/Technique
Date Started:	☐ Seed ☐ Clone

Marijuana Type: ☐ Indica ☐ Sativa ☐ Hybrid

Cannabis Seeds: ☐ Feminized ☐ Autoflower ☐ Regular ☐ CBD

Plant Count	Date Harvested	Date Begin	Date End Cure

AROMA

Bud Density

Loose   50 %   Dense

Trichome Color

White   50 %   Amber

APPEARANCE

NOTES

FEEDING SCHEDULE

	Milliliter	Tablespoon		Teaspoon	
Week #	1	2	3	4	5
Growth Stage					
PPM Range					

NOTES

Reservoir/Bucket Size:				Optimal pH:		
6	7	8	9	10	11	12

NOTES

Strain Name:	Method/Technique
Date Started:	☐ Seed ☐ Clone

Marijuana Type: ☐ Indica ☐ Sativa ☐ Hybrid

Cannabis Seeds: ☐ Feminized ☐ Autoflower ☐ Regular ☐ CBD

Plant Count	Date Harvested	Date Begin	Date End Cure

AROMA

Bud Density

Loose   50 %   Dense

Trichome Color

White   50 %   Amber

APPEARANCE

NOTES

FEEDING SCHEDULE

	☐ Milliliter	☐ Tablespoon	☐ Teaspoon		
Week #	1	2	3	4	5
Growth Stage					
PPM Range					

NOTES

Reservoir/Bucket Size:				Optimal pH:		
6	7	8	9	10	11	12

NOTES

Strain Name:	Method/Technique
Date Started:	☐ Seed ☐ Clone

Marijuana Type: ☐ Indica   ☐ Sativa   ☐ Hybrid

Cannabis Seeds: ☐ Feminized ☐ Autoflower ☐ Regular ☐ CBD

Plant Count	Date Harvested	Date Begin	Date End Cure

AROMA

Bud Density

Loose   50 %   Dense

Trichome Color

White   50 %   Amber

APPEARANCE

NOTES

FEEDING SCHEDULE

	Milliliter	Tablespoon		Teaspoon
Week #	1	2	3	4	5
Growth Stage					
PPM Range					

NOTES

Reservoir/Bucket Size:				Optimal pH:		
6	7	8	9	10	11	12

NOTES

Strain Name:	Method/Technique
Date Started:	☐ Seed ☐ Clone

Marijuana Type: ☐ Indica   ☐ Sativa   ☐ Hybrid

Cannabis Seeds: ☐ Feminized ☐ Autoflower ☐ Regular ☐ CBD

Plant Count	Date Harvested	Date Begin	Date End Cure

AROMA

Bud Density

Loose   50 %   Dense

Trichome Color

White   50 %   Amber

APPEARANCE

NOTES

Feeding Schedule

	☐ Milliliter	☐ Tablespoon		☐ Teaspoon	
Week #	1	2	3	4	5
Growth Stage					
PPM Range					

Notes

Reservoir/Bucket Size:				Optimal pH:		
6	7	8	9	10	11	12

NOTES

Strain Name:	Method/Technique
Date Started:	☐ Seed ☐ Clone

Marijuana Type: ☐ Indica ☐ Sativa ☐ Hybrid

Cannabis Seeds: ☐ Feminized ☐ Autoflower ☐ Regular ☐ CBD

Plant Count	Date Harvested	Date Begin	Date End Cure

AROMA

Bud Density

Loose   50 %   Dense

Trichome Color

White   50 %   Amber

APPEARANCE

NOTES

FEEDING SCHEDULE

	☐ Milliliter	☐ Tablespoon		☐ Teaspoon	
Week #	1	2	3	4	5
Growth Stage					
PPM Range					

NOTES

Reservoir/Bucket Size:				Optimal pH:		
6	7	8	9	10	11	12

NOTES

Strain Name:	Method/Technique
Date Started:	☐ Seed　　☐ Clone

Marijuana Type:　☐ Indica　　☐ Sativa　　☐ Hybrid

Cannabis Seeds:　☐ Feminized ☐ Autoflower ☐ Regular ☐CBD

Plant Count	Date Harvested	Date Begin	Date End Cure

AROMA

Bud Density

Loose　　　50 %　　　Dense

Trichome Color

White　　　50 %　　　Amber

APPEARANCE

NOTES

FEEDING SCHEDULE

	☐ Milliliter	☐ Tablespoon		☐ Teaspoon	
Week #	1	2	3	4	5
Growth Stage					
PPM Range					

NOTES

Reservoir/Bucket Size:				Optimal pH:		
6	7	8	9	10	11	12

NOTES

Strain Name:	Method/Technique
	☐ Seed ☐ Clone
Date Started:	

Marijuana Type: ☐ Indica   ☐ Sativa   ☐ Hybrid

Cannabis Seeds: ☐ Feminized ☐ Autoflower ☐ Regular ☐ CBD

Plant Count	Date Harvested	Date Begin	Date End Cure

AROMA

Bud Density

Loose	50 %	Dense

Trichome Color

White	50 %	Amber

APPEARANCE

NOTES

FEEDING SCHEDULE

	☐ Milliliter	☐ Tablespoon		☐ Teaspoon	
Week #	1	2	3	4	5
Growth Stage					
PPM Range					

NOTES

Reservoir/Bucket Size:				Optimal pH:		
6	7	8	9	10	11	12

NOTES

Strain Name:	Method/Technique
Date Started:	☐ Seed ☐ Clone

Marijuana Type: ☐ Indica ☐ Sativa ☐ Hybrid

Cannabis Seeds: ☐ Feminized ☐ Autoflower ☐ Regular ☐ CBD

Plant Count	Date Harvested	Date Begin	Date End Cure

AROMA

Bud Density

Loose 50 % Dense

Trichome Color

White 50 % Amber

APPEARANCE

NOTES

FEEDING SCHEDULE

	☐ Milliliter	☐ Tablespoon		☐ Teaspoon	
Week #	1	2	3	4	5
Growth Stage					
PPM Range					

NOTES

Reservoir/Bucket Size:				Optimal pH:		
6	7	8	9	10	11	12

NOTES

Strain Name:	Method/Technique
Date Started:	☐ Seed ☐ Clone

Marijuana Type: ☐ Indica   ☐ Sativa   ☐ Hybrid

Cannabis Seeds: ☐ Feminized ☐ Autoflower ☐ Regular ☐ CBD

Plant Count	Date Harvested	Date Begin	Date End Cure

AROMA

Bud Density

Loose   50 %   Dense

Trichome Color

White   50 %   Amber

APPEARANCE

NOTES

FEEDING SCHEDULE

	☐ Milliliter		☐ Tablespoon		☐ Teaspoon
Week #	1	2	3	4	5
Growth Stage					
PPM Range					

NOTES

Reservoir/Bucket Size:				Optimal pH:		
6	7	8	9	10	11	12

NOTES

| Strain Name: | Method/Technique |
| Date Started: | ☐ Seed ☐ Clone |

Marijuana Type: ☐ Indica ☐ Sativa ☐ Hybrid

Cannabis Seeds: ☐ Feminized ☐ Autoflower ☐ Regular ☐ CBD

Plant Count	Date Harvested	Date Begin	Date End Cure

AROMA

Bud Density

Loose   50 %   Dense

Trichome Color

White   50 %   Amber

APPEARANCE

NOTES

FEEDING SCHEDULE

	☐ Milliliter	☐ Tablespoon		☐ Teaspoon	
Week #	1	2	3	4	5
Growth Stage					
PPM Range					

NOTES

Reservoir/Bucket Size:				Optimal pH:		
6	7	8	9	10	11	12

NOTES

Strain Name:	Method/Technique
Date Started:	☐ Seed ☐ Clone

Marijuana Type: ☐ Indica ☐ Sativa ☐ Hybrid

Cannabis Seeds: ☐ Feminized ☐ Autoflower ☐ Regular ☐ CBD

Plant Count	Date Harvested	Date Begin	Date End Cure

AROMA

Bud Density

Loose   50 %   Dense

Trichome Color

White   50 %   Amber

APPEARANCE

NOTES

FEEDING SCHEDULE

Week #	☐ Milliliter	☐ Tablespoon	☐ Teaspoon		
	1	2	3	4	5
Growth Stage					
PPM Range					

NOTES

Reservoir/Bucket Size:				Optimal pH:		
6	7	8	9	10	11	12

NOTES

Strain Name:	Method/Technique
Date Started:	☐ Seed ☐ Clone

Marijuana Type: ☐ Indica ☐ Sativa ☐ Hybrid

Cannabis Seeds: ☐ Feminized ☐ Autoflower ☐ Regular ☐ CBD

Plant Count	Date Harvested	Date Begin	Date End Cure

Aroma

Bud Density

Loose   50 %   Dense

Trichome Color

White   50 %   Amber

Appearance

Notes

FEEDING SCHEDULE

	☐ Milliliter	☐ Tablespoon		☐ Teaspoon	
Week #	1	2	3	4	5
Growth Stage					
PPM Range					

NOTES

Reservoir/Bucket Size:				Optimal pH:		
6	7	8	9	10	11	12

NOTES

| Strain Name: | Method/Technique |
| Date Started: | ☐ Seed ☐ Clone |

Marijuana Type: ☐ Indica ☐ Sativa ☐ Hybrid

Cannabis Seeds: ☐ Feminized ☐ Autoflower ☐ Regular ☐ CBD

Plant Count	Date Harvested	Date Begin	Date End Cure

AROMA

Bud Density

Loose   50 %   Dense

Trichome Color

White   50 %   Amber

APPEARANCE

NOTES

FEEDING SCHEDULE

	☐ Milliliter	☐ Tablespoon		☐ Teaspoon	
Week #	1	2	3	4	5
Growth Stage					
PPM Range					

NOTES

Reservoir/Bucket Size:				Optimal pH:		
6	7	8	9	10	11	12

NOTES

Strain Name:	Method/Technique
Date Started:	☐ Seed ☐ Clone

Marijuana Type: ☐ Indica ☐ Sativa ☐ Hybrid

Cannabis Seeds: ☐ Feminized ☐ Autoflower ☐ Regular ☐CBD

Plant Count	Date Harvested	Date Begin	Date End Cure

AROMA

Bud Density

Loose   50 %   Dense

Trichome Color

White   50 %   Amber

APPEARANCE

NOTES

FEEDING SCHEDULE

	☐ Milliliter	☐ Tablespoon		☐ Teaspoon	
Week #	1	2	3	4	5
Growth Stage					
PPM Range					

NOTES

Reservoir/Bucket Size:				Optimal pH:		
6	7	8	9	10	11	12

NOTES

Strain Name:	Method/Technique
Date Started:	☐ Seed ☐ Clone

Marijuana Type: ☐ Indica   ☐ Sativa   ☐ Hybrid

Cannabis Seeds: ☐ Feminized ☐ Autoflower ☐ Regular ☐ CBD

Plant Count	Date Harvested	Date Begin	Date End Cure

AROMA

Bud Density

Loose   50 %   Dense

Trichome Color

White   50 %   Amber

APPEARANCE

NOTES

FEEDING SCHEDULE

	☐ Milliliter	☐ Tablespoon		☐ Teaspoon	
Week #	1	2	3	4	5
Growth Stage					
PPM Range					

NOTES

Reservoir/Bucket Size:				Optimal pH:		
6	7	8	9	10	11	12

NOTES

Strain Name:	Method/Technique
Date Started:	☐ Seed ☐ Clone

Marijuana Type: ☐ Indica   ☐ Sativa   ☐ Hybrid

Cannabis Seeds: ☐ Feminized ☐ Autoflower ☐ Regular ☐ CBD

Plant Count	Date Harvested	Date Begin	Date End Cure

AROMA

Bud Density

Loose   50 %   Dense

Trichome Color

White   50 %   Amber

APPEARANCE

NOTES

FEEDING SCHEDULE

	☐ Milliliter		☐ Tablespoon	☐ Teaspoon	
Week #	1	2	3	4	5
Growth Stage					
PPM Range					

NOTES

Reservoir/Bucket Size:				Optimal pH:		
6	7	8	9	10	11	12

NOTES

Strain Name:	Method/Technique
Date Started:	☐ Seed ☐ Clone

Marijuana Type: ☐ Indica ☐ Sativa ☐ Hybrid

Cannabis Seeds: ☐ Feminized ☐ Autoflower ☐ Regular ☐ CBD

Plant Count	Date Harvested	Date Begin	Date End Cure

AROMA

Bud Density

Loose   50 %   Dense

Trichome Color

White   50 %   Amber

APPEARANCE

NOTES

FEEDING SCHEDULE

	Milliliter	Tablespoon	Teaspoon		
Week #	1	2	3	4	5
Growth Stage					
PPM Range					

NOTES

Reservoir/Bucket Size:				Optimal pH:		
6	7	8	9	10	11	12

NOTES

Strain Name:	Method/Technique
Date Started:	☐ Seed ☐ Clone

Marijuana Type: ☐ Indica   ☐ Sativa   ☐ Hybrid

Cannabis Seeds: ☐ Feminized   ☐ Autoflower   ☐ Regular   ☐ CBD

Plant Count	Date Harvested	Date Begin	Date End Cure

AROMA

Bud Density

Loose   50 %   Dense

Trichome Color

White   50 %   Amber

APPEARANCE

NOTES

FEEDING SCHEDULE

	☐ Milliliter	☐ Tablespoon		☐ Teaspoon	
Week #	1	2	3	4	5
Growth Stage					
PPM Range					

NOTES

Reservoir/Bucket Size:				Optimal pH:		
6	7	8	9	10	11	12

NOTES

Strain Name:	Method/Technique
Date Started:	☐ Seed ☐ Clone

Marijuana Type: ☐ Indica ☐ Sativa ☐ Hybrid

Cannabis Seeds: ☐ Feminized ☐ Autoflower ☐ Regular ☐ CBD

Plant Count	Date Harvested	Date Begin	Date End Cure

AROMA

Bud Density

Loose   50 %   Dense

Trichome Color

White   50 %   Amber

APPEARANCE

NOTES

FEEDING SCHEDULE

	☐ Milliliter	☐ Tablespoon		☐ Teaspoon	
Week #	1	2	3	4	5
Growth Stage					
PPM Range					

NOTES

Reservoir/Bucket Size:				Optimal pH:		
6	7	8	9	10	11	12

NOTES

Strain Name:	Method/Technique
Date Started:	☐ Seed ☐ Clone

Marijuana Type: ☐ Indica ☐ Sativa ☐ Hybrid

Cannabis Seeds: ☐ Feminized ☐ Autoflower ☐ Regular ☐ CBD

Plant Count	Date Harvested	Date Begin	Date End Cure

AROMA

Bud Density

Loose   50 %   Dense

Trichome Color

White   50 %   Amber

APPEARANCE

NOTES

FEEDING SCHEDULE

	☐ Milliliter	☐ Tablespoon		☐ Teaspoon	
Week #	1	2	3	4	5
Growth Stage					
PPM Range					

NOTES

Reservoir/Bucket Size:				Optimal pH:		
6	7	8	9	10	11	12

NOTES

Strain Name:	Method/Technique
Date Started:	☐ Seed ☐ Clone

Marijuana Type: ☐ Indica ☐ Sativa ☐ Hybrid

Cannabis Seeds: ☐ Feminized ☐ Autoflower ☐ Regular ☐ CBD

Plant Count	Date Harvested	Date Begin	Date End Cure

AROMA

Bud Density

Loose   50 %   Dense

Trichome Color

White   50 %   Amber

APPEARANCE

NOTES

FEEDING SCHEDULE

	Milliliter	Tablespoon	Teaspoon		
Week #	1	2	3	4	5
Growth Stage					
PPM Range					

NOTES

Reservoir/Bucket Size:				Optimal pH:		
6	7	8	9	10	11	12

NOTES

Made in the USA
Coppell, TX
14 April 2022

76575103R00063